The Refuge Vow
A Sourcebook

The world takes refuge in mountains,
Forests and shrines,
Groves and stones,
And deities of trees:
But these are no proper asylum.

Father or mother are no refuge for you,
Neither are friends nor relatives;
Having forsaken you
They depart just as they like.

Take now your refuge in the Buddha,
The Dharma and all the Sangha,
Who eradicate fear in the frightened
And who protect the unprotected.

They who take refuge in the Three Jewels
Will gain fearlessness.

—from *The Jewel Ornament of Liberation*

The Refuge Vow

A Sourcebook

VAJRADHATU PUBLICATIONS

VAJRADHATU PUBLICATIONS
3008 Oxford Street, Suite 201
Halifax, Nova Scotia B3L 2W5
www.shambhalashop.com
Email: orders@shambhalashop.com
(902) 421-1550 Ext. 1

ISBN 1-55055-021-7
PRINTED IN CANADA

Library and Archives Canada Cataloguing in Publication

The refuge vow : a sourcebook.

Includes bibliographical references.
ISBN 1-55055-021-7

1. Vows (Buddhism). 2. Refuge.

BQ4355.R43 2005   294.3'444   C2005-906310-6

CONTENTS

The Refuge Formula

I take refuge in the Buddha.
I take refuge in the dharma.
I take refuge in the sangha.

Becoming a Refugee

Venerable Chögyam Trungpa Rinpoche

Becoming a refugee is acknowledging that we are groundless, and it is ac-knowledging that there is really no need for home, or ground. Taking refuge is an expression of freedom, because as refugees we are no longer bounded by the need for security. We are suspended in a no-man's land in which the only thing to do is to relate with the teachings and with ourselves.

In the Buddhist tradition, the purpose of taking refuge is to awaken from confusion and associate oneself with wakefulness. Taking refuge is a matter of commitment and acceptance and, at the same time, of openness and freedom. By taking the refuge vow we commit ourselves to freedom.

There is a general tendency to be involved in all kinds of fasci-nations and delusions, and nothing very much ever takes root in one's basic being. Everything in one's life experience, concerning spirituality or anything else, is purely a matter of shopping. Our lives consist of problems of pain, problems of pleasure, problems of points of view—problems about all kinds of alternatives—which make our existence complicated.

We have allegiance to "that" and allegiance to "this." There are hundreds and millions of choices involved in our lives particularly in regard to our sense of discipline, our ethics, and our spiritual path. People are very confused in this chaotic world about what is really the right thing to do. There are all kinds of rationales, taken from all kinds of traditions and philosophies. We may try to combine all of them together; sometimes they conflict, sometimes they work together harmoniously. But we are constantly shopping, and that is actually the basic problem.

1

It is not so much that there is something wrong with the traditions that exist around us; the difficulty is more our own personal conflict arising from wanting to have and to be the best. When we take refuge we give up some sense of seeing ourselves as the good citizen or as the hero of a success story. We might have to give up our past; we might have to give up our potential future. By taking this particular vow, we end our shopping in the spiritual supermarket. We decide to stick to a particular brand for the rest of our lives. We choose to stick to a particular staple diet and flourish on it.

When we take refuge we commit ourselves to the Buddhist path. This is not only a simple but also an extremely economical approach. Henceforth we will be on the particular path that was strategized, designed, and well thought-out twenty-five hundred years ago by the Buddha and the followers of his teaching. There is already a pattern and a tradition; there is already a discipline. We no longer have to run after that person or this person. We no longer have to compare our lifestyle with anybody else's.

Once we take this step, we have no alternatives; there is no longer the entertainment of indulging in so-called freedom. We take a definite vow to enter a discipline of choicelessness—which saves us a lot of money, a lot of energy, and lots and lots of superfluous thinking.

Perhaps this approach may seem repressive, but it is really based on a sympathetic attitude toward our situation. To work on ourselves is really only possible when there are no sidetracks, no exits. Usually we tend to look for solutions from something new, something outside: a change in society or politics, a new diet, a new theory. Or else we are always finding new things to blame our problems on, such as relationships, society, what have you. Working on oneself, without such exits or sidetracks, is the Buddhist path. We begin with the hinayana approach—the narrow path of simplicity and boredom.

By taking refuge, in some sense we become homeless refugees. Taking refuge does not mean saying that we are helpless and then handing all our problems over to somebody or something else. There will be no refugee rations, nor all kinds of security and dedicated help. The point of becoming a refugee is to give up our attachment to basic security. We have to give up our sense of home ground, which is illusory anyway. We might have a sense of home ground as where we were born and the way we look, but we don't actually have any home, fundamentally speaking. There is actually no solid basis of security in one's life. And because we don't have any home ground, we are lost souls, so to speak. Basically we are completely lost and confused and, in some sense, pathetic.

These are the particular problems that provide the reference point from which we build the sense of becoming a Buddhist. Relating to being lost and confused, we are more open. We begin to see that in seeking security we can't grasp onto anything; everything continually washes out and becomes shaky, constantly, all the time. And that is what is called life.

So becoming a refugee is acknowledging that we are homeless and groundless, and it is acknowledging that there is really no need for home, or ground. Taking refuge is an expression of freedom, because as refugees we are no longer bounded by the need for security. We are suspended in a no-man's land in which the only thing to do is to relate with the teachings and with ourselves.

The refuge ceremony represents a final decision. Acknowledging that the only real working basis is oneself and that there is no way around that, one takes refuge in the Buddha as an example, in the dharma as the path, and in the sangha as companionship. Nevertheless, it is a total commitment to oneself. The ceremony cuts the line that connects the ship to the anchor; it marks the beginning of an odyssey of loneliness. Still, it also includes the inspiration of the preceptor—in this case myself—and his (or her) lineage. The participation of the preceptor is a kind of guarantee that you will not be getting back into the question of security as such, that you will continue to acknowledge your aloneness and work on yourself without leaning on anyone. Finally you become a real person, standing on your own feet. At that point, everything starts with you.

This particular journey is like that of the first settlers. We have come to no-man's land and have not been provided with anything at all. Here we are, and we have to make everything with our own bare hands. We are, in our own way, pioneers: each is a historical person on his or her own journey. It is an individual pioneership of building spiritual ground. Everything has to be made and produced by us. Nobody is going to throw us little chocolate chips or console us with goodies. So we have to learn how to milk the cows. In fact, we have to find the cows first—they might be wild animals at this point—and we have to tame them, put them into a corral, milk them, and nurse their young. We have to learn how to make a sword: we have to melt the stone and make iron out of it. We have to make everything. We came here barefoot and naked, and we even have to make our own clothes—our own shoes and hats, whatever we need. This is the starting point, right here at this point. It is necessary to make this beginning.

If we adopt a prefabricated religion that tells us exactly the best way to do everything, it is as though that religion provides a complete home with wall-to-wall carpeting. We get completely spoiled. We don't have to put out any effort or energy, so our dedication and devotion have no fiber. We wind up complaining because we didn't get the deluxe toilet tissue that we used to get. So at this point, rather than walking into a nicely prepared hotel or luxurious house, we are starting from the primitive level. We have to figure out how we are going to build our city and how we are going to relate with our comrades who are doing the same thing.

We have to work with the sense of sacredness and richness and the magical aspect of our experience. And this has to be done on the level of our everyday existence, which is a personal level, an extremely personal level. There are no scapegoats. When you take refuge you become responsible to yourself as a follower of the dharma. You are isolating yourself from the rest of your world in the sense that the world is not going to help you any more; it is no longer regarded as a source of salvation. It is just a mirage, maya. It might mock you, play music for you, and dance for you, but nevertheless the path and the inspiration of the path are up to you. You have to do it. And the meaning of taking refuge is that you are going to do it. You commit yourself as a refugee to yourself, no longer thinking that some divine principle that exists in the holy law or holy scriptures is going to save you. It is very personal. You experience a sense of loneliness, aloneness—a sense that there is no savior, no help. But at the same time there is a sense of belonging: you belong to a tradition of loneliness where people work together.

You might say: "I have been this way for a long time. Why does there have to be a ceremony?" The ceremony is important because then there will be a particular time and a date on which your commitment takes place. There will be one particular fraction of a second after which you are committed to yourself, and you will know that very precisely and clearly. It is the same as celebrating the New Year: when the clock strikes twelve, we finally say "Happy New Year." There is that particular moment. So we make sure that there are no fuzzy edges to your memory or commitment. You are a slippery fish, and you have to be provided with some kind of net. The net is the situation of taking refuge that you are caught in; and the fisherman, the person who fishes you out of the water, is the preceptor. At that point the fish has no choice but to surrender to the fisherman. Without the ceremony, somehow it doesn't work; the whole thing is left too much to your imagination and your slippery subjectifying process.

When you become a refugee, a follower of the Buddha's teaching, you get onto a train that is without reverse and without brakes. The train comes along and pulls up to a certain station at a certain time. You get onto the train, then the whistle toots and off you go.

So the refuge ceremony is a landmark of becoming a Buddhist, a nontheist. You no longer have to make sacrifices in somebody else's name, trying to get yourself saved or to earn redemption. You no longer have to push yourself overboard so that you will be smiled at by that guy who watches us, the old man with the beard. As far as Buddhists are concerned, the sky is blue and the grass is green—in the summer, of course. As far as Buddhists are concerned, human beings are very important and they have never been condemned—except by their own confusion, which is understandable. If nobody shows you a path, any kind of path, you're going to be confused. That is not your fault. But now you are being shown the path and you are beginning to work with a particular teacher. And at this point nobody is confused. You are what you are, the teachings are what they are, and I am what I am—a preceptor to ordain you as Buddhist persons. This is a very joyous situation as far as I am concerned: we are going to work together from the beginning to the end.

Taking refuge in the Buddha as an example, taking refuge in the dharma as the path, and taking refuge in the sangha as companionship is very clean-cut, very definite, very precise, and very clear. People have done this for the past twenty-five hundred years of the Buddhist tradition. By taking refuge you receive that particular heritage into your own system; you join that particular wisdom that has existed for twenty-five hundred years without interruption and without corruption. It is very direct and very simple.

Taking Refuge in the Buddha

You take refuge in the Buddha not as a savior—not with the feeling that you have found something to make you secure—but as an example, as someone you can emulate. He is an example of an ordinary human being who saw through the deceptions of life, both on the ordinary and spiritual levels. The Buddha found the awakened state of mind by relating with the situations that existed around him: the confusion, chaos, and insanity. He was able to look at those situations very clearly and precisely. He disciplined himself by working on his own mind, which was the source of all the chaos and confusion. Instead of becoming an anarchist and blaming society, he worked on himself and he attained what is known as *bodhi*, or enlightenment. The final and ultimate breakthrough took place, and he was able to teach and work with sentient beings without any inhibition.

The example of the Buddha's life is applicable because he started out in basically the same kind of life that we lead, with the same confusion. But he renounced that life in order to find the truth. He went through a lot of religious "trips." He tried to work with the theistic world of the Hinduism of the time, and he realized there were a lot of problems with that. Then, instead of looking for an outside solution, he began working on himself. He began pulling up his own socks, so to speak, and he became a buddha. Until he did that, he was just a wishy-washy spiritual tripper. So taking refuge in the Buddha as an example is realizing that our case history is in fact completely comparable to his, and then deciding that we are going to follow his example and do what he did.

By taking refuge you begin to realize that you can actually compete with the Buddha. You can do that. Twenty-five hundred years ago one person, who also had to deal with his daily living situation, managed to awaken himself and experience the pain of life. He was able to work through that and work along with it and finally attain buddhahood, enlightenment. That person was called Gautama, the chief of the Shakya tribe. He was a prince who had all kinds of luxury and security and who felt alienated from his basic state of sanity. So he decided to question the whole thing. He escaped from his kingdom, and he practiced meditation in the jungles and the woods. The only friends or spiritual teachers he could find were all spiritual materialists: they were using meditation to fortify ego. He tried all kinds of physical gimmicks—holding his breath, turning upside down, sitting in the middle of a campfire—and he found them all futile. Then he began to rouse himself, to make his own liberation by himself. So he won enlightenment single-handedly. He was such a smart person that he was able to get out of the psychological materialism of trying to shore up ego through ideas, and out of spiritual materialism as well. He was able to win a victory over both kinds of materialism. Henceforth he was known as the Buddha, the Awakened One.

We can do that as well. Thousands of people in the Buddha's tradition have done so. We have psychological materialism happening constantly in our lives, so we have the same material to work on. There is no doubt that we have plenty of that kind of food for our minds.

One of the big steps in the Buddha's development was his realization that there is no reason we should believe in or expect anything greater than the basic inspiration that exists in us already. This is a nontheistic tradition: the Buddha gave up relying on any kind of divine principle that would descend on him and solve his problems. So taking refuge in the Buddha in no way means regarding him as a god. He was simply a person who practiced, worked, studied, and experienced things personally. With that in mind, taking refuge in the Buddha amounts to renouncing misconceptions about divine existence. Since we possess what is known as *buddha nature*, enlightened intelligence, we don't have to borrow somebody else's glory. We are not all that helpless. We have our own resources already. A hierarchy of divine principles is irrelevant. It is very much up to us. Our individuality has produced our own world. The whole situation is very personal.

Taking Refuge in the Dharma

Then we take refuge in the *teachings* of the Buddha, the dharma. We take refuge in the dharma as path. In this way we find that everything in our life situation is a constant process of learning and discovery. We do not regard some things as secular and some things as sacred, but everything is regarded as truth—which is the definition of dharma. Dharma is also *passionlessness*, which in this case means not grasping, holding on, or trying to possess—it means nonaggression.

Usually, the basic thread that runs through our experience is our desire to have a purely goal-oriented process: everything, we feel, should be done in relation to our ambition, our competitiveness, our one-upmanship. That is what usually drives us to become greater professors, greater mechanics, greater carpenters, greater poets. Dharma—passionlessness—cuts through this small, goal-oriented vision, so that everything becomes purely a learning process. This permits us to relate with our lives fully and properly. So, taking refuge in the dharma as path, we develop the sense that it is worthwhile to walk on this earth. Nothing is regarded as just a waste of time; nothing is seen as a punishment or as a cause of resentment and complaint.

This aspect of taking refuge is particularly applicable in America, where it is quite fashionable to blame everything on others and to feel that all kinds of elements in one's relationships or surroundings are unhealthy or polluted. We react with resentment. But once we begin to do that, there is no way. The world becomes divided into two sections: sacred and profane, or that which is good and proper and that which is regarded as a bad job or a necessary evil. Taking refuge in the dharma, taking a passionless approach, means that all of life is regarded as a fertile situation and a learning situation, always. Whatever occurs—pain or pleasure, good or bad, justice or injustice is part of the learning process. So there is nothing to blame; everything is the path, everything is dharma.

That passionless quality of dharma is an expression of *nirvana*—freedom, or openness. And once we have that approach, then any spiritual practice we might go through becomes a part of the learning situation, rather than merely ritualistic or spiritual, or a matter of religious obligation. The whole process becomes integral and natural.

We have always tried to make sense out of the looseness and unsatisfactoriness of life by trying to make things secure and trying to freeze that washed-out quality into some definite story line. But now we can no longer make very much sense out of it. Things constantly change, constantly move, constantly become something else. So now we begin to work with the basic premise that that flow, or fluctuation of ups and downs, in our lives can be seen as a mirror reflection, or as waves in the ocean. Things come close to us and we can almost hold onto them, but then they disappear. Things seem as if they are just about to make sense; then suddenly there is immense confusion and what was about to make sense seems quite remote, a million miles away. We are constantly trying to grasp something, and we lose it just as we think we have our fingertips on it. This is the source of frustration, suffering—or *duhkha*, as the Buddha called it. Duhkha is the First Noble Truth. Recognizing that, we begin to make sense out of nothing, so to speak. Transitoriness begins to become more meaningful than trying to freeze truth into a solid lump. That realization—understanding the fluctuation that goes on and working with it—is the meaning of taking refuge in the dharma.

This approach involves a quality of directness and absence of deception—or we might even say absence of politeness. It means that we actually face the facts of life directly, personally. We do not have to come up with any padding of politeness or ordinary cheapness, but we actually experience life. And it is very ordinary life: pain is pain and pleasure is pleasure. We don't have to use another word or innuendo. Pain and pleasure and confusion—everything takes place very nakedly. We are simply ordinary. But nakedness and absence of politeness don't necessarily mean being completely savage. We are naked just in going without the padding that we usually provide ourselves with. With our friends, with our relatives, in everything that goes on, we can afford to be very simple and direct and personal.

In that way all the things that go on in life—economic, domestic, and spiritual—are no longer regarded as belonging in separate compartments, but everything is combined into one situation. That is what it means to follow the path of the dharma. Neither hot, intense moments of complete claustrophobia nor cool, noncaring moments are regarded as either extraordinarily good or extraordinarily terrible. Those are just the fashions of life that we are involved in. It is a natural process taking place constantly. Taking refuge in the dharma means relating to everything that happens, from the splinter in your little finger to your granddad's committing suicide in your name, from the littlest to the biggest, as part of that natural process. There are all sorts of shapes of journeys taking place constantly. And all of them are just a trick; they are just interesting facets of life.

But still you can't just say, "Let's leave it alone. Let's just watch everything and become great poets." Oh no. You can't just write poems about it, play music about it, or dance to it. You have to get into all those facets of life completely. And getting into them is the meaning of path—they become the path. That is accompanied by the practice of meditation, which actually makes the whole thing very clear and precise. The clearer our minds become, the more real and vivid become all the little things that are promising and threatening: the hopes and fears, the pains and pleasures.

The dharma is traditionally divided into two aspects. The first is *what has been told*, which means the holy scriptures, the books of the teachings which have been written from the time of the Buddha until the present. Those sacred books, which have been handed down from generation to generation, contain the truth of *what has been experienced*, which is the second aspect of the dharma. Throughout the Buddhist lineage, individuals have experienced reality and truth within the teachings, and this can also be experienced by you. It is a discovery within your own life that happens both with your teacher and by yourself. It happens particularly through your experience of meditation, both in formal sitting practice and in meditation-in-action.

Taking refuge in the dharma means that the experiences that go through your life, pain and pleasure alike, are also sacred teachings. The teachings are not sacred because they were discovered in space or because they came from the sky and were given by divine principles. But the teachings were discovered in the heart, in human hearts—in buddha nature. For example the Buddhist canon, the *Tripitaka*, is based on *somebody's* experience. It is all *somebody's* discourse. The one hundred and eight volumes of sutras are spoken words—communications from one human being to another. The Buddha, who was fully awakened, was communicating with other human beings who were not awakened, were half-awakened, or were in a somewhat-awakened state. The truth has never come from the sky; it has always come from the human condition. The Four Noble Truths of the Buddha describe the human experience of pain, the origin of pain, the possibilities of salvation, and the possibilities of the path. These are very literal truths; they are the direct truth, rather than something that was manufactured upstairs.

So in taking refuge in the dharma, the books of the teachings are not regarded as mystical writings that were created by the clouds and the sun meeting together and engraving script on a tablet. These books were written with ink and pen on pieces of paper. The memories of the seminars, talks, and discourses that Lord Buddha gave were recorded simply as a description of what an awakened man said, how an awakened person conducted himself in the living situation. So taking refuge in the dharma has nothing to do with unearthly influence; it has nothing to do with Martians, and it has nothing to do with Jehovah either—but it definitely has something to do with sanity. Taking refuge in the dharma means that human beings' experience can be heightened so much that, extraordinarily, we can actually awaken ourselves within ourselves.

Once again, whatever goes on in our minds is a learning situation: the love and hate relationships that evolve around us, the sense of misfortune, the sense of being lucky, the sense of defeat, the sense of arrogance and egohood, the sense of patriotism, the sense of smartness, the sense of being special, and the sense of confusion—all are included in our particular basic situation. That is the path. It is the only way; it is the only thing that we can work on. We cannot just milk the cow of the guru all the time, whenever we are hungry or thirsty. But we can experience our lifestyle and our process of development according to the dharma of what has been told. Then we become in tune with the dharma of what has been experienced at the same time, as the followers of the dharma have done in the past—which is very powerful and very meaningful for all of us.

Taking Refuge in the Sangha

Having taken refuge in the Buddha as an example and the dharma as path, then we take refuge in the sangha as companionship. That means that we have a lot of friends, fellow refugees, who are also confused, and who are working with the same guidelines as we are. Everybody is simultaneously struggling with their own discipline. As the members of the sangha experience a sense of dignity, and their sense of taking refuge in the Buddha, dharma, and sangha begins to evolve, they are able to act as a reminder and to provide feedback for each other. Your friends in the sangha provide a continual reference point which creates a continual learning process. They act as mirror reflections to remind you or warn you in living situations. That is the kind of companionship that is meant by *sangha*. We are all in the same boat; we share a sense of trust and a sense of larger-scale, organic friendship.

At the same time, you have to stand on your own two feet. A sense of individuality and a sense of comradeship are both involved. You are working together and helping each other, but you are not helping so much that you become addicted to each other's help. If you lean on somebody in a weak moment of your life, the person you lean on may seem strong, but he will also begin to catch your weakness. If he falls down, you will fall down too. If the principle were just to lean on one another, we could have thousands of people all leaning on each other, but then if one person fell down, everybody would fall down. The whole thing would collapse, like an old dilapidated building, and there would be great chaos. It would be a suicidal process, with thousands all collapsing at the same time—which would be very messy, very dusty.

So taking refuge in the sangha means being willing to work with your fellow students—your brothers and sisters in the dharma—while being independent at the same time. That's a very important point here, actually, in terms of taking the refuge vow. Nobody imposes his or her heavy notions on the rest of the sangha. If one particular person tries to act as a catalyst or spokesman for the whole sangha, that is regarded as frivolous. If someone is extremely timid, credulous, and dependent, that is also regarded as frivolous. Instead, each member of the sangha is an individual who is on the path in a different way from all the others. It is because of that that you get constant feedback of all kinds: negative and positive, encouraging and discouraging. These very rich resources become available to you when you take refuge in the sangha, the fellowship of students. It is as though yeast is put into a batch of hundreds of grains of barley. Each grain begins to fill up with yeast, until finally there is a huge, beautiful, gigantic vat of beer. Everything is yeasted completely; each one of the grains has become powerful individually—so the whole thing becomes a real world.

The sangha is the community of people who have the perfect right to cut through your trips and feed you with their wisdom, as well as the perfect right to demonstrate their own neurosis and be seen through by you. The companionship within the sangha is a kind of clean friendship—without expectation, without demand, but at the same time, fulfilling.

The sangha are a source of learning as much as the spiritual friend or teacher. So there is a need for some trust in the sangha. But we have to make a very definite point here: we are speaking of the *organized* sangha, which is the sangha of practitioners who actually sit together, practice together, and also work on themselves. Without that sangha, we have no reference point; we are thrown back into the big samsaric soup, and we have no idea who or what we are. We are lost.

So we no longer regard ourselves as lone wolves who have such a good thing going on the side that we don't have to relate with anybody at all, whether the organization, the sitting practice, or the sangha at large. At the same time we must not simply go along with the crowd. Either extreme is too secure. The idea is one of constantly opening, giving up completely. There is a lot of need for giving up.

Joining the particular club of lonely people who call themselves the sangha is a very heroic thing to do. Conventionally, you don't join anything unless all the ground is secured. Normally you pay a certain amount of money to join a particular club, and that gives you the kind of service that makes you feel good and secure. But at this point it is a very impersonal approach; in a strange way it is also very personal. You are willing to work with your loneliness in a group. The sangha is made up of thousands of people who are alone together, working together with their own loneliness, their own aloneness. Together they make an orchestra; you are able to dance with its music, and that is a very personal experience. You begin to join that particular energy, which allows individuality and spontaneity as well as nonaggression.

The sense of trust and frankness in the sangha frightens a lot of people; nevertheless, genuine communication takes place. Also, the level of sophistication of the sangha naturally becomes heightened. We cannot regard the sangha as an in-group situation, like a cheap, greasy spoon household of brown-rice eaters. At this level the sangha is an immaculate household, with immaculate relationships, in which experiences with each other occur personally. The real sangha is made up of dedicated people who are actually working on themselves. They haven't developed any fantastic tricks, magic, extraordinary philosophy, or anything like that. From that point of view, such companionship might seem somewhat boring, too ordinary. Nevertheless, it is very real. Quite possibly, you might occasionally seek out extraordinary friends and pursuits, but somehow those pursuits turn out to be purely plastic, part of a dream world, so that you return to the real sangha, the real people who actually care about themselves, care about you as a friend, and relate with the whole situation completely, without any areas shielded through a consensus of weakness.

Having taken the refuge vow, there are three types of change that take place: change of attitude, change of mark, and change of name.

Change of Attitude

Change of attitude involves developing a sense of sympathy toward oneself, and therefore toward the world. One's attitude changes to that of nonaggression and passionlessness. Aggression refers to a general sense of uptightness and unfriendliness—of regarding the world as an object to do battle with. And in passion, one is trying to win something over, engaging in continual one-upmanship. In either case one has a constant battle going on with the world—that is to say, with oneself.

When you change your attitude you develop an awareness that allows you to be friendly with yourself and thus with the rest of sentient beings. There is some sense of gentleness. This is connected with commitment to the practice of meditation, which creates an openness to your own ups and downs, and a willingness to go along with them and work on them. You develop such a thorough relationship with the teachings that they become part of you. The three jewels—the Buddha, the dharma, and the sangha—become a part of your existence and you thrive on that, you work with that, you live on that. You do not become a religious person as such, but you become gentle, soft, and very amiable and workable. You don't create defense mechanisms all the time.

As a Buddhist, you are less greedy. If your breakfast isn't cooked just the way you want it, you give in and eat the crummy breakfast you don't like. There is a sense that you can give an inch in your demands—just a little inch, a fraction of a second. So trying to give in, which is the change of attitude, is very important. Usually we don't want to give in: "I want to have my own way. I want complete, one hundred percent hospitality; and if I don't get it, I'm going to fight for my rights," and so forth. This is problematic and anti-Buddhist in some sense.

Another aspect of the change of attitude is that when you become a full-fledged Buddhist you feel that your life is workable in any situation. You don't feel alienated from your problems, and you don't try to put yourself in some kind of special spiritual orbit. You can be very gentle and friendly to yourself and other people and relate with the world—which seems to be the basic point of the Buddhist teachings. But you don't have to conduct yourself with the superficial smile and gleaming, honey-smeared attitude of "love and light." This is a genuine experience: you enter the tradition of the nonaggressive state of mind, and you are capable of conducting yourself in that way without artifice.

Nonaggression in this context also means refraining from taking life; you refrain from the personal rejection of animals, enemies, human beings, or whatever. People sometimes take pride in killing flies; in that kind of little situation they become involved in some kind of "gotcha!" mentality. That's a very savage kind of behavior. Becoming a follower of the dharma means becoming more sophisticated in the fundamental sense. You begin to pay attention to the details of your daily life situation, which become more important, and in fact sacred.

Such an attitude cannot be made up. It only comes from lots of meditation practice; that seems to be the only way. The sitting practice of meditation seems to produce gentleness and compassion naturally.

Change of Mark

Change of mark is closely related to change of attitude. Once you begin to behave with nonaggression, you begin to show signs of the sanity that is already in you. You don't actually have to try to prove anything to your relatives, your parents, your friends. The words don't count; the people around you can simply and actually appreciate the development of gentleness and reasonableness taking place in you. It is not that you are trying to be polite and understanding in the cheap sense, but you are trying to be polite and understanding beyond consideration of your own personal comfort. So some sense of gentleness and sympathy takes place, and that is the mark of being Buddhist. You begin to turn into a different breed of person. You become gentle and considerate, and open and brave at the same time.

You are not suddenly going to become a glowing, happy, easy-going, enlightened person, obviously. But the whole idea is that it is possible, if one's sitting practice and discipline are taking place, that one's personality could change from that painful, serious, deep-down level of neurosis into something open, sharp, profound, and delightful. This is not particularly a salesman's pitch—that change has been happening to students throughout the whole of our experience in this country.

Change of Name

Traditionally, in Tibet and other Buddhist countries, the parents would give their child a nickname that was used during childhood.

Then, when the child took the refuge vow, they would be given a Buddhist name. The nickname would be phased out, or maybe just used occasionally among one's close circle of relatives, and the Buddhist name would then be assumed. In this setting, that situation may be somewhat sticky, so I like to leave it up to each person whether or not they want to use their refuge name. The point is that when you are called by your Buddhist name, you should assume that particular attitude of gentleness. Your name should act as a reminder rather than as something that provides further identification for your ego or that is just purely a handle.

The meaning behind the name is connected with some kind of inspiration that you might develop. It is not necessarily a flattering name, nor is it condescending—but it is some kind of message. Your Buddhist name represents an encouragement for some kind of development in your personality, which is connected with the practice of meditation—some sense of your individual style in approaching the dharma.

The Refuge Vow Ceremony
The main part of the refuge vow ceremony involves offering three prostrations then repeating the refuge formula three times: "I take refuge in the Buddha, I take refuge in the dharma, I take refuge in the sangha." I should explain the purpose of prostrations. There are all kinds of self-made spiritual journeys that we might be able to take, but what is important and necessary is to surrender our ego trips. Such surrender makes us much more self-made and much more closely and personally related with reality. So the idea of the prostrations is to surrender your personal clingings of all kinds so that you can begin to tune in to this particular path.

When you prostrate you hold your palms together successively at the level of your forehead, your throat, and your heart, which represents surrendering your body, speech, and mind to the Buddha, dharma, and sangha without expecting anything in return.

Prostrating on the ground is very significant; it means surrendering finally. You are making a real commitment; you are willing to give in completely to the choiceless sanity of the earth and become a refugee in no-man's land. The past, present, and future lineage holders are represented by this earth. You may get pissed off at this earth; you may feel very good about this earth; you may feel very unconcerned about this earth—but still the earth remains here, and it remains solid. Bowing yourself down on this earth is surrendering yourself to this basic sanity.

You do the three prostrations to the shrine, which represents our heritage. More explicitly, it represents the lineage of those who transmit awakened mind, which exists in the past, present, and future. You are also prostrating to the preceptor, who is the inheritor of this lineage. The method used in the past is no longer a myth, but is real and living. You have a living Buddhist in front of you.

Kneeling and repeating the refuge formula three times is the actual refuge-taking. It has three aspects: acknowledging oneself, acknowledging one's need for protection, and acknowledging the other. When you say, "I take refuge," you are requesting to be accepted as a refugee. And when you say, "in the Buddha, dharma, sangha," you are acknowledging the other, which is the example, the path, and the sense of community. In this situation you have to be very deliberate, precisely aware of all the processes you are going through.

You repeat the refuge formula three times. The first time is preparing the ground; the second time you are going further; and the third time you have actually gone completely.

The discipline of taking refuge is something more than a doctrinal or ritual thing: you are being physically infected with commitment to the buddhadharma; Buddhism is transmitted into your system. Something in the lineage which is very physical, almost at the level of chemistry, enters your heart as your commitment to openness takes place. The third time you say, "I take refuge in the sangha," the preceptor snaps his fingers. That is the moment of real transmission. At that moment the sperm, so to speak, enters your system and you become part of the lineage. From that moment onward, you are a follower of the practicing lineage of the Kagyü. At that particular point, the energy, the power, and the blessing of basic sanity that has existed in the lineage for twenty-five hundred years, in an unbroken tradition and discipline from the time of Buddha, enters your system, and you finally become a full-fledged follower of buddhadharma. You are a future living buddha at that point.

Taking Refuge
Venerable Chögyam Trungpa Rinpoche

On taking refuge the first rule, which is general to all schools of Buddhism, is to know how to respect the triple gem and how to develop a proper sense of reverence. In Tibet, at the same time as first learning to take refuge in Buddha, dharma, and sangha, Buddhists are also taught the following rules; even the ordinary householders teach their children that these rules are to be respected and obeyed at all times.

The first three rules are prohibitions:
Having taken refuge in the Buddha, do not seek refuge in gods who still dwell in the samsaric plane as they themselves are not free from attachment and suffering.

Having taken refuge in the dharma, do no harm to any beings, nor speak against other religions because these too contain some ethical codes.

Having taken refuge in the sangha, do not consort with people of bad behavior or worldly habits.

The next three rules contain positive instruction:
Taking refuge in the Buddha includes paying respect to the buddha-rupa or to any other holy image, also to any part of it, broken or otherwise. It should be handled respectfully and with due reverence and never be trodden on (even accidentally) or thoughtlessly picked up (especially not by the head).

In the same way, taking refuge in the dharma includes reverential treatment and respect of books. These should never be used thoughtlessly or as props for other articles. This respect for the scriptures extends to those of other faiths and languages.

Taking refuge in the sangha includes respect to all Buddhist priests not only for themselves but for what they represent. Also respect for one's teacher is considered very important.

Mahayana lays special emphasis on reverential behavior to the guru who is regarded as the representative of the Lord Buddha himself, and who gives personal guidance to his pupil.

This reverence and esteem for the guru goes even further, for in his Buddha aspect he is accepted as the representative of the triple gem in its entirety. The mind of the guru is the mind of Buddha as he participates (1) in the realization of the buddha nature; (2) has perception of the buddha mind in the higher levels of meditation; (3) has experience of teaching and the distribution of knowledge combined with extreme compassion for his pupils' human weaknesses and failings; and (4) has accumulated this spiritual power for the benefit of all mankind.

The guru's speech is the dharma in that he has attained high levels in meditation and can convey this knowledge to his pupils, leading and guiding them to the truth. Spiritual power is also conveyed in his voice, which has the capacity to dispel ignorance.

The guru's body is representative of the sangha in that it is the physical vehicle of the teaching.

The mahayana expands the Buddhist teaching of the triple gem by affirming that the buddhas are all comprised under the three kayas: the nirmanakaya ("divine body of incarnation"), sambhogakaya ("divine body of perfect endowment"), and dharmakaya ("divine body of truth"). The dharma is comprised of the three yanas—hinayana, mahayana, and vajrayana—while bhikshus and arhats; bodhisattvas and maha-bodhisattvas; yogins and vidyadharas constitute the three corresponding forms of the sangha.

Whichever form of Buddhism is followed, the observance of these rules is necessary for the development of a proper sense of reverence toward the triple gem. To disregard them can only result in harm to the individual, the building up of bad karma, and the deterioration and eventual loss of religious aptitude, while to follow them will result in greater perception and understanding.

Taking Refuge

The Sakyong, Jamgön Mipham Rinpoche

Here at seminary, we are practicing and trying to understand the teachings of Buddha. Taking refuge is a critical point in that process, so it is wonderful that you have come here to engage in this refuge ceremony. In taking refuge, we make a decision to enter into the practice of buddhadharma—to meditate, to understand the teachings, and to engage in a life in accord with them. In Buddhist countries, taking refuge is taken for granted, but here in the West it is not. Even though at this time Buddhism has become extremely popular, it is still unusual for someone to take refuge.

Taking refuge is the point at which you make a decision: either you are a Buddhist or not. Taking refuge is not a temporary situation; once you take the refuge vow, it lasts forever. Sometimes after taking refuge, people wonder if they made the right decision. Before you choose to become a Buddhist, you can say you are a Buddhist or you are not a Buddhist, or you can also give a neutral answer. After you take the refuge vow, there is only one answer to the question, "Are you a Buddhist?" "Yes, I am a Buddhist." You have entered through a certain gate. You are a Buddhist in the elevator, at the mall, or at a *bar mitzvah*. So it is important to go through the process of deciding whether or not this is what you want to do with your life, and to make a conscious decision. You are not taking refuge for somebody else. It is a personal journey.

In our community, the refuge ceremony represents birth. In life we are born only once, not every week. But with refuge, we are born every day. We should take refuge every single day to clarify what that means. Why? Because taking refuge is really about how we are going to lead our lives. We take refuge because in looking throughout the world for a place where we could be content, where we could reduce our anxiety, we realized that there is really no place or thing that will cause us to be content, to find harmony, or to understand the nature of things.

Refuge in the Buddha

The Buddha lived in a palace and had good food and drink. He did everything that there was to do. If there had been movies, he would have seen them all. Yet something was not quite right. Where was the meaning of life? So the Buddha took refuge in the truth, the dharma. We are taking the same journey as the Buddha. Like the Buddha, we are asking, "Where is our life taking us?" That leads us to taking refuge in the Buddha, the dharma, and the sangha. "Sangha" in Tibetan is *gendün. Ge* means virtue; it's used here like the word *vira* in Sanskrit, or *virtus* in Latin. It also means *pawo*, "warrior." Those who are in the sangha are warriors, because they are trying to come out of samsara. They are willing to break their habits, no longer doing the same thing over and over. Habits are not just made up of combing your hair or dressing in a certain way. Habits have to do with the mind getting perpetually stuck in trying to find peace, happiness, stability, or contentment. We take refuge because we finally realize that in order to find those things, we cannot look outside; we have to look inside.

The Buddha looked inside to understand the mind, and we use the Buddha as an example. We look at the Buddha with a sense of respect and appreciation for showing us how to live our life. This is not a theistic situation in which Buddha is better and we are worse, or he is the boss and we are the servants. Buddha is not a god. Buddha is us. We are Buddha, but we have not yet realized our full buddhahood. When we take refuge in the Buddha, we take shelter from confusion, chaos, and suffering. We actually have to *think* about taking refuge. We have to *feel* it.

When we talk about Buddha, in Tibetan we say *chom-den-de. Chom* means "to destroy" or "to overcome." The Buddha overcame his tendency to always think about himself first. He was able to overcome his kleshas and see beyond ego. He realized that there is really no self. In a sense, there is a person who rides on a bus or washes dishes—but the Buddha realized that the self we hang onto so tightly does not really exist. In overcoming our kleshas, our discursiveness, we too can begin to step out of our self-involvement and start thinking about others. From a greater point of view, the Buddha overcame not just the notion of self, but also of phenomena. He realized the egolessness of self and of other, destroying such conceptuality as "I'm here and you're there," and the continual world of duality. The Buddha was obviously quite a smart chap, quite the thinker.

The word *den* means "to possess." The Buddha possesses wisdom, compassion, and power. Following this path gives us wisdom so we know what we are doing; compassion so that we are able to have a soft heart and care about others; and power in the sense of continuing to go on the journey. *De* means "gone beyond." We usually think that Buddhism means going to nirvana, a sense of peace and contentment, but the Buddha's realization is beyond that. He has gone beyond samsara and nirvana, beyond existence, beyond nihilism and eternalism. We call him the Buddha because he awoke and was actually able to see. He is often depicted as having a third eye. We can only see so much out of two eyes. We also need the eye of wisdom. When we take refuge in the Buddha, we are taking refuge in the qualities of the Buddha that are inherent within us. We call that buddha nature. We are not taking refuge in *me*, in ego; we are taking refuge in intrinsic enlightenment, and we are becoming part of a bigger family of Buddhists.

Refuge in the Dharma

This leads us to the dharma, which is the second aspect of taking refuge. It is fine to have the Buddha, but what is most important and instrumental is not so much who the Buddha was, but what he

29

expressed: a fearless proclamation of the truth, the dharma. It takes a long time to understand what the Buddha taught. When the Buddha said there was no self, most people did not want to listen.

When we begin to meditate, we realize that our idea of who we are is partly created by who our friends are. We see that what we think about is who we know, where we want to go, and where we just came from. We have created this individual in relationship to other. At a certain point, our mind begins to relax, our thoughts begin to disappear, and we may become a bit frightened. We think we're going crazy. Our sense of boundary begins to dissolve. There is no one to talk to, because there is no one there. We realize we are really holding on to our conceptualization—the idea of who we are and what we want. Everything we engage in is conceptualization. We have a concept about something and, in a few years, our concept has changed. We say, "That was the old me, and now I am a different person." A few years later, we have changed again. To follow the Buddhist path, we have to look inside our own mind. The dharma helps us do that. The process of meditation helps us go beyond concept and realize the truth.

The dharma is seamless. It says the same thing over and over again. Maybe you have had the experience of opening a book on dharma, and it just happens to fall open to the right page. You exclaim, "That's exactly what is going on! That's me. That's my problem right now." If the dharma began to change, then it would no longer be the dharma. It would no longer be the truth. How can the truth change? Truth has to be constant.

The dharma provides stability in our life. It is something that we can reflect upon as we jump all around. It protects our mind and it protects our heart. We take refuge in the dharma because the dharma is the words, the meaning, and the teachings of the truth. By taking refuge in the dharma, we learn what is correct and incorrect. We learn the right view and the ultimate view and how to rely on the dharma in terms of action. When we assimilate and understand the dharma, it becomes like armor that protects us from wrong view and samsara. Can we be fearless? Can we look at what is there or what is not there?

Refuge in the Sangha

Most people have no problem taking refuge in the Buddha, who seems like a nice guy. Dharma also sounds good. What about the sangha? Now it gets personal. We think the sangha is great, except for . . . Everything in the sangha is fine . . . except we wish they would change this or that. This is true in our sangha and other sanghas as well. I know different groups of Buddhist practitioners, and they are always complaining about each other. Some people who come to Shambhala say, "You guys are so organized." To me, this is like a joke. What does the word *organized* mean? Does it resemble *chaos*?" [Laughter] It must mean that when someone says one thing, another person does something else.

The sangha—gendün—is a group of individuals who are on the path with us. *Ge* has to do with virtue. But sangha are not just goody-goodies. *Dün* usually means "aspiration." Sangha are those who aspire every day to deepen their practice of mindfulness, awareness, and compassion. They are people who come together to practice together and who also help each other. As we walk around, we can't see that we are buddha; we see ourselves as ordinary. At the same time, we can take inspiration from one another. It's easy to think that the sangha should be made up of individuals who act in an ideal manner—but if that really happened, what would be the point of sangha? Everybody would already be a buddha. We do not need to become buddhas to have some compassion. We do not have to be buddhas to offer a helping hand. Sangha are those who are supporting and caring for each other. That means you can rest on someone's shoulder.

The sangha is also the container. When we practice together in this tent, the sangha helps our discipline; it helps us to meditate.

31

If we sit by ourselves in our apartment, we can do whatever we want. If we decide to have a cup of tea, we can jump up. If we have an interesting thought, we can go look something up. If we get hungry, we can have a sandwich. When we sit down in the shrine tent, we realize that there are other people around who are going through the same thing. That gives us a feeling of encouragement. The sangha is our literal support.

You would think that Shakyamuni Buddha would have had the best sangha of all, because he was the man of the time. But if the Buddha had had such a great sangha, they would not have needed all those rules. The rules of the vinaya, about how monks and nuns should behave, came about because the sangha did *not* behave. The sangha of the Buddha was composed of monastics. They had temptations, but they didn't have as many distractions. They did not have Fort Collins. They did not have the Potbelly or the High Country [restaurants near RMSC] or the commissary or the bath-house. [Laughter]

The Buddha lived in the forest. There is only so much you can do in the forest. But if we give ourselves enough time, we can always figure out something to do. We like this tree, we do not like that tree. This tree has better shade than that tree. That monk has better shade—tomorrow *I* am going to get that shade. I do not want to wash my bowl downstream from that guy up there. I didn't like the way so-and-so said something. Whatever the situation, that is what happens. Eventually, silence was imposed because everybody was talking too much.

Our time is not so different. We are more technologically advanced and there is much more for the mind to be busy with now. We have television, movies, videos, and the computer. We have cars and planes. Everything happens much more quickly. We can entertain ourselves for a longer duration of time. However, at some point we are going to be stuck in some airport by ourselves and we will be left with—guess who? Us! We will be left with that thing called mind. We regard the mind as problematic. However, as Buddhists, we say that although our mind might be a little wild right now, it is workable. In fact, it is not only workable, it has tremendous potential. In becoming Buddhists, externally we are joining a large group of individuals who practice, but on an inner level, at a certain point it becomes very, very personal.

Entering the Path

As we enter the Buddhist path, it is important that we continue to look deeper and see our life as a vehicle, a way to grow individually and become bigger. It is not difficult to have more anger or more jealousy. That is no big deal. When we do mantras, using our malas, we are trying to understand who we are. But often, rather than sitting and thinking, "OM MANI PADME HUM," we think, "I'm really pissed off, I'm really pissed off, I'm really pissed off." [Laughter] "When's lunch? When's lunch?" "I'm irritated; this is boring; what am I doing?" "I exist, I exist, I exist; let me count the ways." [Laughter] If the point of our path was to get as upset or irritated as we could, practice would be easy. We could all be buddhas. But we are talking about taking a special route—"the path less traveled." This path has been traveled well by many people, many great practitioners. It is now up to us to travel this path.

This is a completely possible situation. There is no reason that we cannot travel this path. We all have our own situations or karma. Some of us tend to be more lazy. Some of us tend to be more uptight. Some of us tend to be a little more intellectual. Some want to work or be more physical. We all have various tendencies. But the truth remains the same—unchanging. That is the beauty of the dharma. It is completely available. We don't have to do any particular hoo-hah in order to understand that. On the other hand, we do need to hear, meditate, and contemplate. We do need to understand what we are doing. We do need to correct our misunderstandings. The dharma is a very personal journey. Nobody else can label that thought for you. Nobody else can deal with that emotion for you. You have to work it out for yourself.

We take refuge in the Buddha, dharma, and sangha, which are known as the triple gem, the three precious jewels. Taking refuge is something that we have to initiate. That is why we have this ceremony: it marks the time, the day, and the place where we actually stepped onto that path. Some of you may feel that you have been Buddhists your whole life, but it is still important to declare it to yourself and others. In the refuge ceremony, we make that statement to ourselves in front of the community. Once we take refuge, on one hand we are still whoever we are; on the other hand, there is a kind of transformation. However, as we know, there are all kinds of Buddhist people. It is really up to us how we would like to travel this journey.

Taking refuge does not mean that we take Buddha's words as the unquestioned truth. We must question the words of the Buddha. We must read the dharma, try to understand it, and practice it. We need to ask, "Is this real? Does this actually work? Does it make sense?" Buddha did not say, "I am going to save you." He said, "You have the ability to make your situation better. You have all the capabilities. It is up to you. I will help as much as I can." You can lead a horse to water, but you can't make him drink. We have to drink the water of dharma ourselves.

I don't want to be too heavy-handed, because this is supposed to be a cheerful occasion. It is really wonderful what you are doing.

[REFUGE CEREMONY]

Studying the Dharma

It takes a while to understand Buddhist logic and analysis. Sometimes you feel really stupid, like the whole thing is not working. We are beginning to mold our view of the world. The logics that are presented are quite stunning. You do not study Buddhist logic in the same way you study a lot of other things. We are not using just our intellect, but we are beginning to look at phenomena, at ourselves, and at our practice in a different way. When we study the twelve nidanas, for example, we want to get it but we don't quite get it. We get part of it and not another part. So we get upset with ourselves.

When we move into madhyamaka, it gets so deep. We are used to thinking about things in a certain way—and this is another way. We are going along one road and the dharma is going along another. So we try to figure out how to cross over into the other lane, but it does not quite happen. However, the more soaked we are in the dharma, the more we begin to understand the logic of the dharma, the more the roads begin to come together. When we do vajrayana practice and begin to read sadhanas, we begin to understand what is being presented. We would like to say, "I got it. Let's move on." There *is* something to get, obviously, and there *is* something we can understand, but we are not trying to get something. We would like to think we have gotten it—"Yeah, I got it!"—and then two days later it is gone. We cannot remember what the *subject* was, let alone what the *details* were.

When you study dharma, at some times it is blissful and wonderful; at others, it is like doing surgery on yourself—uncomfortable, claustrophobic, or irritating. You get upset at the teachings, the teacher, or the whole situation. Some people have not heard this kind of language before. It takes a while to get familiar with it. Some people say, "This is not what the Vidyadhara said in this or that book. It does not correlate." But if you go back and look closely at what he is saying, it *will* correlate. I have read the same books that he read, and I know what he was trying to explain. When you try to figure it out, you realize that sometimes he is not talking technically, but from an experiential point of view. However, there is still logic in that. Once you soak yourself in the dharma, you begin to realize how you are reacting to it, which is part of the process. When people said, "That was wonderful, but I didn't understand it," the Vidyadhara would tell them to go back and study some more. The point is, the dharma is the dharma.

Refuge & Precepts

Khenchen Thrangu Rinpoche

The second aspect of the foundation for developing the mentality of enlightenment is the refuge. You may have been practicing the dharma for quite a long time and have taken refuge in the Three Jewels a long time ago. However, this is the section in *The Jewel Ornament* when this is explained. Some might feel that taking refuge is very elementary because you have heard about it often and done it a long time ago, but it might be very meaningful to look at refuge once again. Refuge is something that we will need all the time until we accomplish Buddhahood. From the moment we take refuge until we become a Buddha, we will still remain exposed to the sufferings of existence and will still need protection; we will still need the protection of refuge.

When we speak about refuge it has two aspects; it is possible to see it in two different ways. There is what is known as "the cause refuge" and "the result refuge." Result refuge is the more important of the two.

While we are in conditioned existence we have all sorts of fears, problems, difficulties and sufferings. All other beings also experience this. When will all this stop? When will the time come when we need not be afraid of suffering? It will only come when we accomplish Buddhahood. But the accomplishment of Buddhahood depends upon ourselves; it is entirely up to us whether we accomplish Buddhahood or not. If we try it is impossible not to succeed and if we don't try then there is no possibility to succeed. Even if we practiced towards Buddhahood while all beings in the universe were armed against us, still they couldn't prevent us from accomplishing Buddhahood. On the other hand, if we do not practice and all beings in the universe tried to help us, we couldn't achieve it. It depends entirely upon us whether we become a Buddha or not.

Becoming a Buddha means transcending all suffering and all the fears one has of suffering. It means eliminating all the negative aspects and revealing or manifesting all the qualities of Buddhahood. Yet all of this is something that is taking place within our mind. This is the reason why we have to work on our own mind by eliminating all faults and negative aspects and work on our own mind to make all the qualities manifest and bring them to full fruition.

When we achieve the ultimate fruit, we achieve the transcendence of all forms of suffering; it is the time of real refuge as perfect protection, the ultimate form of refuge.

Result refuge speaks of refuge in the ultimate sense. Cause refuge is the refuge in the temporary sense; it is the refuge that we need to work on, refuge in the Buddha, the dharma and the sangha. The Buddha is the one who shows us the path, the dharma is the path itself, and the sangha are the friends and companions who help us on the path. Refuge is an entire chapter in this book and consists of nine points: classification, working basis, the object, the time, the motivation, the procedure, the function, the precepts, and the benefits.

1. The Classification. The first point describes the classification of refuge, which has two aspects. These two aspects are conditioned by our meditation and by the quality of our attitude. If we are taking refuge for our own benefit, with a self-centered motivation, then refuge is common. If we are taking refuge for the benefit of all other beings that have been our parents in previous lives then refuge is special.

2. The Working Basis. The second point concerns the basis for refuge, which is what kind of individual is considered the basis of refuge. Again we find two aspects, the common working basis and the special working basis. The individual as a common base is someone who will take common refuge, who seeks refuge out of fear of the suffering of conditioned existence. The individual as a special base are those who take special refuge and who possess the mahayana potential and wish to bring all beings to enlightenment; such individuals have a very high and pure motivation.

3. The Object. The third point in the chapter on refuge describes the object of refuge, the ones we take refuge in. Again, there is a twofold division into the common and the special object.

The common object of refuge is threefold: There is refuge in the Buddha who represents the very best realization and the very best possible purity arising from having eliminated all faults. There is refuge in the second object, which is the dharma, the scriptures of the words of the Buddha as well as the realization of the teachings. The third object of refuge is the sangha, the sangha of ordinary beings and the sangha of realized beings. These are the Three Jewels or Three Rare and Precious Ones who are the objects of common refuge.

The special object of refuge is also threefold: The first are objects abiding directly in front of us. The second is the object of direct realization, the object when really understood. The third is the ultimate object of refuge, suchness. The first objects of refuge are objects that are present and near us. This will be the Buddha (images of the Buddha), the dharma (the Mahayana scriptures) and the sangha (the community of bodhisattvas).

We were not present 2,500 years ago when the Buddha Shakyamuni was present and teaching in the world and we could not see him with the thirty-two special marks and eighty special signs. One could think, "Well, I didn't have the good karma to see him. Maybe I had the wrong karma and missed the chance. Since I missed the chance there is nothing I can do and therefore I cannot practice." However this isn't true. It makes no difference whether you meet Buddha Shakyamuni or not because the main thing, as already mentioned, is that practicing the teachings depends on nobody but us, not even on the presence of the Buddha. It depends upon us alone whether we practice or not and whether we are able to generate the necessary qualities of faith, of respect and devotion, of courage and diligence, and of understanding.

If we can have faith and devotion in the Buddha then this is something that will immediately give us the sufficient determination to practice the path. Faith in the Buddha is explained here in terms of very deep appreciation for what Buddha stands for, to acknowledge his great qualities for what they are. Once we acknowledge this, once we appreciate these qualities, we will have profound respect and great reverence for the Buddha. But more than that, we will have the aspiration to achieve the same thing ourselves. And out of this aspiration we will want to practice as intensively and strongly as we can. This will give rise to diligence. And once we have diligence, automatically understanding will arise. So, in this case, the Buddha must be seen as the one who can generate in us the feeling of intensive faith, devotion, and the aspiration to practice.

The present case we are discussing is that of the Buddha as a material representation; it can be a statue or painting. But in any case, we shouldn't think that this representation is merely a material object, like a piece of paper or cloth or clay. We shouldn't look down on it but realize that it is the symbolic representation of the Buddha and as such it is something that can help generate the faith and aspiration we need to really practice the path. In this sense it makes no difference whether we met the Buddha when he was alive or not because the pure and perfect mind of the Buddha is never far away from beings. If somebody has faith, there is no difference whether the Buddha is near or far, present or not, or only in the form of a representation. The essential point is to develop the right faith and aspiration. This concerns the Buddha as the object in front of us.

The dharma is represented in the form of books that teach the dharma. As mentioned, we didn't have the opportunity to hear the

Buddha speak the teachings during his life but we have the teachings in writing; we have all the books that convey the dharma. And these books are not just ordinary books. They are the written words that can bring us to find the very best possible form of happiness; they convey the deepest meaning and therefore we must regard them with sincere respect. This is the dharma in the form of the object in front of us, represented by the scriptures.

The sangha in front of us refers to the sangha consisting of ordinary beings, which includes our dharma friends. We shouldn't look at the sangha as ordinary friends because these are the friends on the extraordinary path to enlightenment.

So, these three objects are the objects in front of us, the visible objects.

The second aspect of the object of refuge is the object of direct realization. It is the Buddha who possesses the nature of the three kayas, the one who is the dharmakaya, the sambhogakaya, and the nirmanakaya. The dharma of direct realization is the very nature of peace, the nature of what is beyond suffering, and this is nirvana. The sangha of direct realization are the realized bodhisattvas who are on the bodhisattva levels. This is the object of refuge in the light of direct realization.

The third aspect of refuge is the ultimate object of refuge. This goes back to what was mentioned earlier. Ultimately, Buddhahood is the refuge; when one becomes a Buddha it is real refuge. So refuge in the ultimate sense is becoming Buddha oneself, referred to as real refuge.

This concludes the section on the object of refuge, the common and the special refuge.

4. The Time. The fourth point explains the duration of refuge. Concerning common refuge, we take refuge for this life only, until our death. Concerning the special refuge, we take refuge from now until we accomplish full and perfect enlightenment, until we accomplish Buddhahood.

5. The Motivation. The fifth point describes the mental attitude for taking refuge, of which there are two types. In common refuge, one takes refuge in order to be protected from samsara for oneself. In special refuge, one takes refuge in order to be able to protect all other living beings from suffering.

6. The Ceremony. The sixth point describes the procedure of taking refuge. As previously explained, the main difference between the two forms of refuge is simply a difference of motivation. As far as the ceremony is concerned, the main thing is to repeat after the teacher the formula of taking refuge; one repeats after him that one is taking refuge in the Three Jewels. But repeating the words of refuge after the teacher should not only be a formal matter; it shouldn't just be a repetition of words. When one promises to take refuge it should come from deep within and be done sincerely and purely.

7. The Function. The seventh point describes the function of refuge. In the short term, the function of taking refuge is to find protection from the three lower states of existence (the result of the common refuge). In ultimate terms, it is to find protection from all the suffering of conditioned existence in samsara through accomplishing buddhahood (the result of the special refuge).

8. The Training. The eighth point describes the training and practice that follow the ceremony of taking refuge. The practice and training are there to help us work towards Buddhahood. When someone has taken refuge their situation has changed. What has changed is the necessity to engage in certain things and to avoid others in order to bring refuge to life and to realize it. If we follow these practices it is a sign that something has changed.

There are nine practices to train in, which are divided into three groups of three: Three general trainings, three specific trainings and three common trainings. The first group pertains to all of the Three Jewels as a whole. The second set pertains to each of the Three

Jewels specifically. The third pertains to the extension of the Three Jewels, to things connected with the Three Jewels.

a) The Three General Trainings. The first set of three practices we must train in apply to the Three Jewels together and in general. The first training is that we should always try to make offerings to the Three Jewels, to the Buddha, to the dharma and to the sangha. Making offerings means to give whatever part of our belongings, possessions or wealth we are ready to give away to the Buddha, to the dharma and to the sangha.

However, we shouldn't misunderstand the nature of offerings. We are not making offerings because the objects of refuge are poor or destitute or in order to please them so that they are nice to us. We shouldn't think that if we don't give them anything they will be very mad at us and throw us into the lower realms of suffering. We are not making offerings for that purpose. We make offerings because the offerings are an expression of great appreciation towards the Three Jewels. We need to develop a great sense of appreciation, confidence, joy, and enthusiasm towards the Three Jewels. In fact, the degree of appreciation, enthusiasm, and confidence we have in the Three Jewels will determine the extent to which our own qualities can develop and increase. Without adequate appreciation, enthusiasm and so on, our qualities will not develop very well. That is why we make offerings, to enhance our joy and enthusiasm for practice and our appreciation of the Three Jewels. If we have a very strong sense of appreciation then we will be able to offer our most precious belongings to the Three Jewels. That is the first training, to continuously strive to make offerings to the Three Jewels.

The second training is to never forsake the Triple Refuge, to never to give up the Three Jewels. We realize that the highest anticipated advantages come from the Three Jewels; there is nothing else that could ever benefit us as the Three Jewels will. That is why we should never give up refuge in the Three Jewels at any cost.

The third training is to always remember the Three Jewels; to always keep the Three Jewels in mind because it is most important for us.

b) The Three Specific Trainings. The second set of three practices we have to train in apply to one of the Three Jewels specifically. The first training has to do with the Buddha. Once someone has taken refuge in the Buddha it is said that he or she should not go for refuge in any worldly god. Upon hearing this some people may find that this is a very sectarian or biased view. Although it might seem to be like this, it isn't so. When it is taught that we should not seek another refuge other than the Buddha it doesn't imply that the Buddha would be jealous and would not protect us. It is taught with respect to the very essence of the Buddha.

How does the Buddha protect us? He gives us the refuge through teaching us the right path, by showing us the right way. If we follow that way we will achieve the ultimate result, which is protection from all suffering. But if we do not follow that path then we cannot expect to be on the right path and to achieve freedom from suffering. So, as long as we take refuge in the Buddha we are on the right path. If we go for refuge in other deities, gods or whatever, then it doesn't mean that the Buddha would be upset or jealous and would stop protecting us, rather automatically we would deprive ourselves of the benefits that come from following the right path, the path shown by the Buddha.

The second training has to do with the dharma. Once someone has taken refuge in the dharma they should give up harming other beings. This may sound like a very difficult thing to do but actually it isn't that hard because, as said before, everything depends upon the quality of our motivation; everything is a matter of the right way of thinking. We should understand that the very essence, the heart of the dharma is the path that frees all beings from suffering. If we harm beings it automatically goes against the very essence of

44

the path of dharma, which is intended to free us from suffering, not bring more suffering. Taking refuge in the dharma automatically implies not harming other beings.

The third training concerns the sangha. It is said that once someone has taken refuge in the sangha they should not associate closely with those who are not in the dharma. We shouldn't misinterpret this to mean not associating closely with others such that we cannot eat, talk, or spend time with them. Instead, it means that we should not adopt their views and behave like they do. Basically, why do we take refuge in the sangha? We take refuge in the sangha because they are the ones who can accompany us on the path and help us to practice properly. If we stop having a close association with sangha members then we won't have refuge in the sangha who can help and support us. If we associate with others then we start taking on their ways. That is the reason why we take refuge in the sangha and associate closely with them, otherwise refuge in the sangha is pointless.

c) **The Three Common Trainings.** The third set of three practices to train in has to do with anything related with the Three Jewels. The first one has to do with what is related to the Buddha. When we take refuge in the Buddha it is out of a sense of great appreciation for what the Buddha stands for and out of respect for his great qualities. You may wonder why we have to consider the Buddha as being so special. If we think of all living beings in general, and ourselves in particular, the only one who can really help us—not only in the immediate future but also ultimately—is the Buddha. Because of his outstanding qualities the Buddha can show the path that leads to ultimate liberation, ultimate happiness. This is a very special quality that no other being has. So, we have great respect for the Buddha and appreciate his excellence because of his outstanding qualities.

Once we know this then we should consider that anything representing the Buddha is an object of respect because it symbolizes the Buddha. If we see anything, a statue, picture or any form of representation of the Buddha, be it small or large, be it of ordinary or precious material, be it broken or only a splinter, we should always treat it as something very special because it represents what can render true protection from suffering and what can lead to ultimate happiness. It represents what can take us out of suffering towards goodness and happiness. This is a quality that we never find in anything else. This isn't a quality we would ever find in the most precious stones like a ruby, lapis-lazuli, or emerald; they won't contain such qualities. But here, even the tiniest fragment of a representation of the Buddha represents for us all the blessings of the Buddha. As explained earlier, what we need is strong appreciation for the qualities of the Buddha as well as sincere respect and aspiration towards them. So, any representation of the Buddha, even a fraction of a representation, can help us to develop this sense of appreciation and aspiration and so as such it should be respected and treated as something very special.

The second training has to do with everything connected with the dharma. The books and texts of the Buddha's teachings explain the path and provide instructions that lead to ultimate liberation and ultimate happiness, Buddhahood. Therefore they are very precious and we should have great respect for even one syllable of these texts.

The third training has to do with everything connected with the sangha. We should consider that anybody who helps us on the path of dharma—even if only to a very tiny extent—is a very special person and someone we have to respect because they are the ones who help us travel on the path to Buddhahood.

This set of instructions reminds us to respect anything that is connected with the Buddha, dharma and sangha.

9. The Beneficial Effects. The ninth point of the chapter on refuge describes the benefits that come from refuge, of which there are eight: we enter the Buddhist path, refuge becomes the foundation for all the other precepts, refuge becomes a cause for purification of all the previous negative actions accumulated, we cannot be affected by obstacles caused by either humans or nonhumans, accomplishing all our wishes, we achieve the great cause of merit, not falling into the lower realms, and we quickly accomplish perfect enlightenment.

We can summarize this into the immediate and ultimate benefits. The immediate benefits are that we are protected from the sufferings of the three lower states. The ultimate benefit is that through taking refuge in the Three Jewels we are protected from all the sufferings of samsara, insofar as this will help us accomplish Buddhahood.

These nine points show us everything we need to know about refuge.

The Pratimoksha Precepts. The third aspect of the foundation for developing the mentality of enlightenment is that one should keep any of the seven forms of the pratimoksha precepts. These are the vows of discipline that are part of what is known as "individual liberation" and can be divided into those for lay and ordained people.

You may wonder why we need one of these vows in order to cultivate bodhichitta. *The Jewel Ornament* gives three reasons why they are needed as a foundation: analogy, scriptural authority, and reasoning.

1. Analogy. We would not invite a great king to reside in a place where there is filth and which is unclean. The place should be clean and decorated with many ornaments. Similarly, the king of bodhichitta cannot be invited to reside where our body, speech and mind are not free from nonvirtue and are stained with the dirt of negative karma. Instead, bodhichitta should be invited to abide where our body, speech and mind are free of the dirt of defilements and are fully adorned with the moral ethics of abandonment.

2. Scriptural Authority. *The Lamp for the Path to Enlightenment* (Tib. *Jangchub Lamgyi Dronma*) says, "One who keeps one of the seven pratimoksha precepts has the fortune to receive the bodhisattva precepts. Otherwise not." Therefore, any of the seven pratimoksha precepts is said to be the foundation.

3. Reasoning. When we take the pratimoksha precepts we abandon causing harm to others and harboring harmful intentions. The bodhisattva's vow causes us to benefit others. Without avoiding harm, there is no method of benefiting others.

This concludes the explanation of the eighth chapter, on taking refuge and precepts, from *The Jewel Ornament of Liberation.*

Remarks on Refuge

Venerable Tsoknyi Rinpoche

There are two kinds of refuge: A personal and private sense of taking refuge which is done when one has an appreciation for the Buddha and for the Buddha's teachings. This personal, informal taking of refuge usually indicates that you want to practice the Buddha's teachings. But if you leave it at that—personal and informal—then somehow there is no strong confirmation of your refuge, and your commitment may stay or it can easily wane. The second kind of taking refuge is done in a formal ceremony, often within a group of people. While taking refuge in the formal sense involves a ritual performed in a group, it is also very personal. But the commitment is made publicly.

In the refuge ceremony, you are acknowledging the Buddha as your teacher, the dharma—his teachings—as the path, and the sangha, the community of those with whom you will follow the teachings of the Buddha. The sangha witnesses your commitment in the refuge ceremony and they stand in support of your practice. There is also the teacher from whom you take the refuge vows and who acts as both witness and preceptor to your aspirations. The teacher officiates over the formal refuge ceremony in which you acknowledge the Buddha as your teacher, and his teaching, the dharma, as your path. As a result of the ceremony you become part of the sangha of those who follow the teachings of the Buddha, the community who helps you walk on the path of the dharma. Therefore, taking refuge in this formal ceremony establishes your commitment; your refuge becomes more official, publicly confirmed, and better established. Taking refuge in this formal way allows you to become a Buddhist. By becoming a Buddhist we mean that you are expressing the wish to practice the teachings of the Buddha.

I was asked in the group discussions the other day if taking refuge entailed becoming religious, or if taking refuge would be like a religious conversion. Whether Buddhism is a religion or not is a bit difficult to say because we have to go to the meaning of the word "religion." Actually, In Buddhist terminology, we just talk about someone being called a practitioner of the dharma. So the word "religion" doesn't really come much into the picture. The main objective of the dharma is to know the essence—the natural state of mind—and to experience and understand absolute reality, or reality as it is. The Buddhist path does have some religious elements that help in this realization—elements such as devotion, compassion, faith, and so forth. But the main objective of the dharma is to know the natural essence. That's the main purpose of the dharma. Whereas in some religions we worship in order to be "reconnected" with the creator after having fallen down from a state of grace, Buddhism talks about being connected with the nature of things, being connected with the true reality. So in order to make that connection one follows the path of the dharma, which, as I explained before, is the dharma of teachings and the dharma of realization. Because one needs the dharma of realization, we need to get involved with the dharma of teachings. So that is what you are taking refuge in. Ultimately, the real meaning of refuge is that you will practice the dharma. There are many benefits in taking refuge, but most importantly, when you take refuge you are committing yourself to practicing the dharma.

After taking refuge there are some things that need to be observed as a discipline. The main observance is you will abstain from the ten wrong-doings[1] as much as you can. You may know that it will be difficult to completely abstain from all of the ten wrong-doings, but you take the attitude that you can do it. In other words, you make the decision that as much as you can you will abstain from them. While there are many benefits in taking refuge, and disadvantages when you don't, the most important benefit comes from committing yourself to practicing the dharma. You are mainly taking refuge in the dharma. So you are ready to change your mind and you're taking refuge from now until attainment of full enlightenment.

Once you take refuge in Buddhism—or in the Buddha, dharma, sangha—then what is the attitude towards other religions and spiritual traditions? Does taking refuge mean that then you have to abandon the other traditions, or that you have to reject them? What it means is that you are now going to devote yourself to the practice of Buddhism. You do not have to reject or abandon other spiritual traditions or consider them negatively and not worthwhile. Instead, you have an attitude of respect for other spiritual traditions. But because your interest is now in Buddhism, you are dedicating yourself to practicing the dharma, but not from a negative point of view. We honor and appreciate other spiritual traditions, but that doesn't mean that we necessarily practice them.

The Buddha was very clear about this: there is a very serious offense in the vajra samaya—the commitments of the vajrayana. One of the fourteen root vows says: "Respect all paths and systems." One breaks that vow if one rejects or deprecates other spiritual traditions. If one demeans another spiritual traditional, then he or she is breaking this root vow. So Buddha was very clear about the seriousness of this kind of offense. The reason for this vajrayana vow is that there are values in other spiritual traditions that are also common to Buddhism. For example, all other spiritual traditions have some aspect of compassion or renunciation. They also have intelligence and insight; they often include faith and devotion. These qualities are all contained within Buddhism also. So to despise other spiritual traditions indirectly means that you are despising or rejecting those qualities that are present in your own Buddhist tradition. This is called "abandoning the dharma."

Once you take refuge, you recognize that while there are many other spiritual traditions, you have decided to follow one way, which is the Buddhist way. You don't say other paths are bad, and you don't despise other spiritual traditions. You have full choice—you may take refuge or you may not take refuge. It's up to you.

Footnotes

[1] The ten wrong-doings or "nonvirtuous actions" are three of body: 1. *killing any sentient being*, 2. *stealing*, 3. *sexual misconduct*; four of speech: 4. *lying*, 5. *slander*, 6. *abusive speech*; 7. *idle chatter and gossip*; and three of mind: 8. *covetousness*, 9. *thoughts of wanting to cause harm to others*, and 10. *wrong view*.

Taking Refuge:

The Foundation Stone of all Paths
Patrul Rinpoche

> *Crowned with the three jewels of the outer refuge,*
> *You have truly realized the three roots, the inner refuge;*
> *You have made manifest the three kayas the ultimate refuge.*
> *Peerless Teacher, at your feet I bow.*

APPROACHES TO TAKING REFUGE[1]

FAITH

Just as taking refuge opens the gateway to all teachings and practices, it is faith that opens the gateway to taking refuge. As the first
step in taking refuge, therefore, it is important to develop a lasting
and stable faith. Faith itself is of three kinds: vivid faith, eager faith,
and confident faith.

Vivid Faith

Vivid faith is the faith that is inspired in us by thinking of the immense compassion of the Buddhas and great teachers. We might
experience this kind of faith on visiting a temple containing many
representations of the Buddhas' body, speech and mind, or after an
encounter with a great teacher or spiritual friend we have just met
personally or whose qualities or life-story we have heard described.[2]

Eager Faith

Eager faith is our eagerness to be free of the sufferings of lower
realms when we hear them described; our eagerness to enjoy the
happiness of higher realms and of liberation when we hear what
they are; our eagerness to engage in positive actions when we hear

what benefits they bring; and our eagerness to avoid negative actions when we understand what harm they cause.

Confident Faith

Confident faith is the faith in the Three Jewels that arises from the depth of our hearts once we understand their extraordinary qualities and the power of their blessings. It is the total trust in the Three Jewels alone that comes from the knowledge that they are the only unfailing refuge,[3] always and in all circumstances, whether we are happy, sad, in pain, ill, living or dead.[4] The Precious Lord of Oddiyana says:

> The faith of total trust allows blessings to enter you.
> When the mind is free of doubt, whatever you wish
> can be achieved.

Faith, then, is like a seed from which everything positive can grow. If faith is absent, it is as though that seed had been burnt. The sutras say:

> In those who lack faith
> Nothing positive will grow,
> Just as from a burnt seed
> No green shoot will ever sprout.

Of the seven noble riches, faith is the most important. It is said:

> The precious wheel of faith
> Rolls day and night along the road of virtue.

Faith is the most precious of all our resources. It brings an inexhaustible supply of virtues, like a treasure. It carries us along the path to liberation like a pair of legs, and gathers up everything positive for us like a pair of arms.

> Faith is the greatest wealth and treasure, the best of legs;
> It is the basis for gathering all virtues, like arms.

The compassion and blessings of the Three Jewels are inconceivable, but nevertheless their ability to reach into us depends entirely on our faith and devotion. If you have immense faith and devotion, the compassion and blessings you receive from your teacher and the Three Jewels will be equally immense. If your faith and devotion are just moderate, the compassion and blessings that reach you will also be moderate. If you have only a little faith and devotion, only a little compassion and blessings will reach you. If you have no faith and devotion at all, you will get absolutely nothing. Without faith, even meeting the Buddha himself and being accepted as his disciple would be quite useless, as it was for the monk Sunakshatra...and for the Buddha's cousin, Devadatta.

Even today, whenever the Buddha is invoked with sincere faith and devotion, he is there, bestowing blessings. For the Buddha's compassion there is no near or far.

> For all who think of him with faith
> The Buddha is there in front of them
> And will give empowerments and blessings.

And the Great Master of Oddiyana says:

> For all men and women with faith in me, I, Padmasambhava,
> Have never departed—I sleep beside their door.[5]
> For me there is no such thing as death;
> Before each person with faith, there is a Padmasambhava.

When one has confident faith, the Buddha's compassion can be present in anything. This is illustrated by the tale of the faithful old woman who was helped towards Buddhahood by a dog's tooth.

Once there was an old woman whose son was a trader. He often went to India on business. The old woman said to him one day: "Bodh Gaya is in India, and that's where the perfectly enlightened Buddha came from. Bring me some special relic from India, so that

I can do my prostrations to it." She repeated her request many times, but her son kept forgetting and never brought her what she had asked for.

One day, as he was preparing to leave again for India, his mother said to him, "This time, if you fail to bring me something for my prostrations, I shall kill myself in front of you!"

The son travelled to India, concluded the business he had planned, and set off back home, once more forgetting his mother's request. It was only as he was nearing his house again that he remembered her words.

"Now what am I going to do?" he thought to himself. "I haven't brought anything for my old mother's prostrations. If I arrive home empty-handed, she'll kill herself!"

Looking around him, he saw a dog's skull lying on the ground nearby. He pulled out one of the teeth and wrapped it in silk. Arriving home, he gave it to his mother, saying, "Here is one of the Buddha's canine teeth. You can use it as a support for your prayers."

The old woman believed him. She had great faith in the tooth, just as if it really were the Buddha's. She did prostrations and offerings all the time, and from that dog's tooth came many miraculous pearls.[6] When the old woman died, there was a canopy of rainbow light around her, and other signs of accomplishment.

Now a dog's tooth does not contain any blessings. But the old woman's faith was so strong that she was sure that it really was the Buddha's tooth. Through her faith the tooth was imbued with the Buddha's blessings, until in the end that dog's tooth was in no way different from a real Buddha's tooth.

Once, in the province of Kongpo, there lived a simple-minded fellow who later became known as Jowo Ben. He made a journey to Central Tibet to see the Jowo Rinpoche.[7]

When he first arrived in front of the statue, there was no caretaker or anyone else about. Seeing the food offerings and the butter lamps in front of it, he imagined that the Jowo Rinpoche must dip pieces of the offering cakes in the melted butter of the lamps and eat them. The wicks were burning in the lamps, he supposed, to keep the butter liquid.

"I think I'd better eat some, like Jowo Rinpoche does," he thought to himself, and dunking a piece of dough from the offering tormas into the butter, he ate it. He looked up at the smiling face of the Jowo.

"What a nice lama you are," he said. "Even when dogs come and steal the food you've been offered, you smile; when the draught makes your lamps sputter, you still keep smiling. Here, I'll leave you my boots. Please look after them for me while I walk around you."[8]

He took off his boots and put them up in front of the statue. While he was circurmambulating round the middle pathway that circles the temple, the caretaker saw the boots. He was about to throw them out when the statue spoke.

"Don't throw those boots away. Kongpo Ben has entrusted them to me!"

Ben eventually came back and took his boots.

"You really are what they call a good lama!" he said to the statue. "Next year, why don't you come and visit us. I'll slaughter an old pig and cook it for you and brew you up some nice old barley beer."

"I'll come," said the Jowo.

Ben went back home and told his wife, "I've invited Jowo Rinpoche. I'm not sure exactly when he's coming, though—so don't forget to keep an eye out for him."

A year went by. One day, as she was drawing water from the river, Ben's wife clearly saw the reflection of Jowo Rinpoche in the water.

Straight away she ran home and told her husband: "There's something down there, in the river... I wonder if it's the person you invited."

Ben rushed down to the river and saw Jowo Rinpoche shining in the water. Thinking that he must have fallen into the river, Ben jumped in after him. As he grabbed at the image, he found that he could actually catch hold of it and bring it along with him.

As they were proceeding towards Ben's house, they arrived in front of a huge rock on the side of the road. The Jowo did not want to go any further.

"I do not enter laypeople's homes," he said, and disappeared into the rock.

This place, to which the Jowo himself was seen coming, is called Jowo Dolé, and the river in which the image appeared bears the name of Jowo River. Even nowadays, it is said that this place confers the same blessing as the Jowo in Lhasa, and everyone does prostrations and makes offerings there. It was by the power of his firm faith that Ben experienced the compassion of the Buddha. Although he ate butter from the lamps and food from the offerings, and put his boots up in front of the Jowo—acts which otherwise could only be wrong—the power of his faith made it all positive.

What is more, it is also upon faith alone that actual realization of the absolute truth, the natural state, depends. It is said in a sutra:

> O Shariputra, absolute truth is only realized through faith.

As you develop a faith quite beyond the commonplace, by its power the blessings of the teacher and of the Three Jewels will enter you. Then true realization will arise and you will see the natural state as it really is. When that happens you will feel an even more extraordinary and irreversible faith and confidence in your teacher and in the Three Jewels. In this way faith and the realization of the natural state support each other.

Before leaving Jetsun Mila, Dagpo Rinpoche asked him when he should start to teach.

"One day," the Jetsun replied, "You will have a realization that brings you an extraordinarily clear vision of the nature of your mind, quite different from the one you have now. At that time, firm faith will arise in you and you will perceive me, your old father, as a real Buddha. That is when you should start to teach."

Our capacity to receive the compassion and blessings of the teacher and the Three Jewels, therefore, depends entirely on devotion and faith.

Once, a disciple called out to the master Jowo Atisha "Jowo, give me your blessing!"

"Lax disciple," Atisha replied, "give me your devotion..."

So absolute unwavering trust, arising from extraordinary faith and devotion, is indispensable. It opens the door to taking refuge.

MOTIVATION

There are three different levels of motivation for taking refuge with this sort of faith.

1. The Refuge of Lesser Beings

Fear of the sufferings of the three lower realms—the hell realm, the preta realm and the animal realm—motivates us to take refuge simply with the idea of obtaining the happiness of gods and men.

2. The Refuge of Middling Beings

The knowledge that wherever we are reborn in any of the realms of samsara, high or low, there is no freedom from suffering, motivates us to take refuge in the Three Jewels just with the aim of attaining for ourselves the level of nirvana, peaceful and free from all samsara's sufferings.

3. The Refuge of Great Beings

The sight of all beings plunged in the great ocean of samsara's infinite sufferings and undergoing an unimaginable variety of torments motivates us to take refuge with the idea of establishing them all in the unsurpassable and omniscient state of perfect and complete Buddhahood.

Of these three levels of motivation, here we should choose the way of great beings, taking refuge out of a desire to establish each one of the whole infinity of beings in the state of perfect Buddhahood.

The happiness of gods and men may seem at first sight to be true happiness. In fact, however, it is not free of suffering; and as soon as the effects of the good actions that lead them to those states of happiness are exhausted, they fall back into lower realms. Why strive to achieve the happiness of higher realms if it only lasts for a moment? The shravakas' and pratyekabuddhas' nirvana brings peace and happiness, but to ourselves alone; when all beings—our mothers and fathers since beginningless time—are sinking in samsara's infinite ocean of sufferings, not to try to help them would not be right. To take refuge in the Three Jewels with the wish that all beings may attain Buddhahood is, therefore, the way of great beings and the gateway to infinite merit. That is the way we, too, should adopt. It is said in the *Jewel Garland:*

> As there are infinite kinds of beings
> The wish to help them is infinite, too.

THE PRECEPTS OF TAKING REFUGE
The precepts consist of three things to be abandoned, three things to be done, and three additional attitudes which are to be observed.

The Three Things To Be Abandoned
Having taken refuge in the Buddha, do not pay homage to deities within samsara. In other words, since the gods of the *tirthikas*[9], like Ishvara or Vishnu, are themselves not liberated from the suffering of samsara, nor are local gods, owners of the ground, or any other powerful worldly gods and spirits, you should not take them as your refuge for future lives, make offerings to them, or prostrate to them.

Having taken refuge in the dharma, do not harm others, even in your dreams. Make vigorous efforts to protect them to the best of your ability.

Having taken refuge in the sangha, do not get involved with tirthikas and other such people who do not believe in the teaching of the Conquerors or in the perfect Buddha who taught it. Although there are no real tirthikas in Tibet, you should also avoid getting involved with anyone who acts like a tirthika—who insults and criticizes your teacher and the dharma, for instance, or who denigrates the profound teachings of Secret Mantrayana.

The Three Things To Be Done
Having taken refuge in the Buddha, honour and respect even a tiny piece of broken statue representing him. Raise it above your head [to carry something on the crown of one's head is to venerate it], put it somewhere clean, have faith, and perceive it with pure vision, considering it as the true jewel of the Buddha.

Having taken refuge in the dharma, respect even a fragment of paper hearing a single syllable of the scriptures. Place it above you head and consider it to be the true jewel of the dharma.

Having taken refuge in the sangha, consider anything that symbolizes it, be it no more than a patch of red or yellow cloth, as the true jewel of the sangha. Honour and respect it, raise it above your head, put it somewhere clean, and regard it with faith and pure vision.

The Three Supplementary Precepts
Look upon your teacher, the spiritual friend who teaches you here and now what to do and what not to do, as the true jewel of the Buddha. Do not even so much as walk on his shadow, and endeavour to serve and honour him.

Consider every word of your sublime teacher as the jewel of the dharma. Accept everything he says without disobeying a single point.

Consider his entourage, his disciples and your spiritual companions who have pure conduct as the jewel of the sangha. Respect them with your body, speech and mind and never upset them, even for an instant.

...So, from the moment you enter the path of liberation and become a Buddhist, practise the taking of refuge along with its precepts, and give them up even if your life is at stake. As a sutra puts it:

> Those who take refuge in the Buddha
> Are true lay followers;
> They no longer should seek refuge
> In any other deity.
> Those who take refuge in the sacred dharma
> Should have no harmful thoughts.
> Those who take refuge in the noble sangha
> Should no longer associate with tirthikas.

These days, some people claim to be followers of the Three Jewels but do not have the slightest respect for their representations. They consider paintings and statues representing the Buddha or books containing words to be ordinary goods that can be sold or pawned. This is "living by holding the three jewels to ransom" and is a very severe fault. To point out the ugliness of a drawing or statue of the Buddha or otherwise criticize it, unless you are evaluating its proportions in order to fix it, is also a grave error and should be avoided. To place books containing the scriptures directly on the floor, to step over them, to wet your fingers with saliva to turn the pages and similar disrespectful behaviour are all serious mistakes as well. The Buddha himself said:

> At the end of the five hundred years
> My presence will be in the form of scriptures.
> Consider them as identical to me
> And show them due respect.

It is an everyday maxim that one should not put images on top of the scriptures. For it is the representation of the speech of the Buddha, rather than that of his body or mind, that teaches us what to do and what not to do and also ensures the continuity of his doctrine. The scriptures are therefore no different from the Buddha himself, and are particularly sacred.

References in footnotes marked 'NT' are taken from *A Guide to The Words of My Perfect Teacher,* by Ngawang Pelzang *(ngag dbang dpal zang),* alias Khenpo Ngakchung, who was the close disciple of Nyoshul Lungtok Tenpai Nyima, himself the close disciple of Patrul Rinpoche. Tibetan text republished by Thubten Nyima, Zenkar Rinpoche, Minorities Publishing House, Chengdu, China. This collection of explanatory notes, which expands in detail selected points from the present text, has been translated into English under the direction of Alla Zenkar Rinpoche (with the participation of members of the Padmakara Translation Group) and is available from Shambhala Publications.

Footnotes

[1] To "take refuge" or "go for refuge" has long been the standard English translation for *skyabs su 'gro ba*. The root meaning is to seek protection from a danger, in this case the dangers of samsaric existence. Why all paths? Because taking refuge is a necessary part of every path of the sutras and tantras.

[2] Here faith is simply a spontaneous response. "In this case, one does not necessarily know the reasons for one's faith." (NT)

[3] "When one has this kind of faith, one knows why. One has faith because one knows that the Three Jewels, and in particular the spiritual teacher, are an infallible refuge." (NT)

[4] This means that our faith in the refuge will enable us to deal with the experiences of the intermediate state *(bar do)* after death.

[5] The word "door" (*sgo*) here refers implicitly to faith, as what gives access to the blessings of the Buddha, of Padmasambhava, or of one's teacher (Pema Wangyal Rinpoche).

[6] *ring bsrel:* round objects like minute pearls which emerge from the relics of realized practitioners.

[7] The famous statue of the Buddha. Princess Wen-Ch'eng Kung-chu, *Kongjo* to the Tibetans, was the daughter of the T'ang emporer Tai-tsung. Upon her marriage to King Songtsen Gampo, she brought to Tibet as part of her dowry a statue of Shakyamuni Buddha at the age of twelve. The Ramoche temple was built in 641 to house it but it was later moved to the Rasa Trulnang (Jokhang), where it is now.

[8] Eating the offerings and putting his boots up in front of the statue would be considered a scandalous act of sacrilege.

[9] Sanskrit for "non-Buddhists." An epithet applied by Buddhist ascetics fo the Brahmans and certain yogis of India.

Recommended Books and Texts

Gampopa. *The Jewel Ornament of Liberation*. Translated and annotated by Herbert V. Guenther. Berkeley: Shambhala Publications, 1971.

Gampopa. *The Jewel Ornament of Liberation*. Commentary by The Venerable Khabje Khenchen Thrangu Rinpoche. Crestone, CO and Auckland, NZ: Namo Buddha Publications and Zhyisil Chokyi Ghatsal Publications, 2003.

Mipham Rinpoche, The Sakyong Jamgön. *Arousing the Motivation for True Freedom from Samsara: The Practice of Taking Refuge*. Halifax: Vajradhatu Publications, 2002.

____. *1999 Seminary Transcripts, Book One*. Halifax: Vajradhatu Publications, 2000.

Patrul Rinpoche. *The Words of My Perfect Teacher*. Translated by the Padmakara Translation Group. Boston: Shambhala Publications, Inc., 1998.

Trungpa, Chögyam. *The Heart of the Buddha*. Boston & London: Shambhala Publications, Inc., 1991.

____. *The Collected Works of Chögyam Trungpa: Volume 1*. Boston & London: Shambhala Publications, 2003.